The Campus History Series

SPRING ARBOR
UNIVERSITY

The Campus History Series

SPRING ARBOR UNIVERSITY

Susan Panak and Robbie Bolton

ARCADIA
PUBLISHING

Published by Arcadia Publishing
Charleston, South Carolina

Printed in the United States of America

Library of Congress Control Number: 2022951717

For all general information, please contact Arcadia Publishing:
Telephone 843-853-2070
Fax 843-853-0044
E-mail sales@arcadiapublishing.com
For customer service and orders:
Toll-Free 1-888-313-2665

Visit us on the Internet at www.arcadiapublishing.com

To all who have walked these hallowed grounds—past, present, and future.

Contents

ACKNOWLEDGMENTS

We are indebted to the many archivists and librarians who have come before us in Spring Arbor. Without those committed to preserving objects of the past in the collective memory of the Spring Arbor University community, this book would not have been possible. Special thanks to historian Howard A. Snyder (1958, 1960), author of Spring Arbor University's history, whose written contribution cannot be understated.

We would like to thank the administration at Spring Arbor University for its support of this project, specifically Pres. Brent Ellis and Matt Gin, assistant vice president for advancement, for seeing the value that this work could bring to Spring Arbor University in commemoration of its 150th anniversary.

We are grateful to David Kohns (2024) for his copyediting of this work, as well as reviewers Shirley Zeller (1984), Jayne Asbury (1966), and Rob Kingsley for providing feedback on early drafts. Special thanks to archival assistant Zoe Reimer (2023) for her meticulous on-demand factchecking.

This book was made possible in part due to the generosity of Frank J. DiSanto. Over 30 years ago, DiSanto provided an endowment to support the work of White Library. A portion of that donation was used to fund this project. We appreciate his generosity.

Robbie (1998) would like to thank his wife, Maria (2004), and his children Rocky, Chet, and Greta for their support and patience with these types of projects he often finds himself in. He also wants to thank Susan for co-laboring with him on this project and tolerating the many delays and tangents of this work.

Susan (2010, 2021) would like to thank her husband, Dave. He patiently waited as she delayed her retirement to work on this final project, one that she could not refuse for her love of Spring Arbor University and its rich history. She would also like to thank her children David, Mallory, and Zachary for their continuous support. Last but not least, she would like to thank Robbie for his support over the years of the archives and digitization efforts.

Finally, we'd like to thank our colleagues in the White Library over the past 20 years. All of them, directly or indirectly, had a hand in the completion of this project. Thank you.

We have truly benefited from a community of learners in crafting this book, and in the words of 1915 yearbook editor John M. Thompson (1915), we "hope that this book may be a pleasing morsel upon the palate of all your varying tastes."

Unless noted otherwise, all images in this book are housed in the Spring Arbor University Archives.

INTRODUCTION

Spring Arbor University (SAU) celebrates its sesquicentennial anniversary in 2023. In May 1873, Spring Arbor Seminary (SAS), predecessor to SAU, opened its doors for a shortened term to 29 primary and intermediary students under the leadership of Clark Jones, the principal, and E.P. Hart, chairman of the board of trustees. Hart and a small group of Free Methodists spearheaded the movement for this "school devoted to the promotion of earnest Christianity and sound, solid learning."

This pictorial history is not a chronological timeline of the historic events of SAU per se. For a written narrative account, consult Howard Snyder's eloquently detailed history of SAU, *Concept and Commitment: A History of Spring Arbor University, 1873–2007*. This narrative is mostly told from the images and artifacts housed in the SAU Archives received from institutional departments, administrators, faculty, and many individual donors—mostly alumni—over the years.

This story chronicles the growth from a seminary, meaning a school of secondary education, to university status. The history of SAU since it attained university status is beyond the scope of this narrative. However, the decision to separate athletics into its own chapter reflects the early institutional ideology that athletic activity is important to "overcome undesirable traits of character" and that it continues to be an important part of university life. The book is organized into the following chapters:

SETTING THE FOUNDATION. A Michigan conference of the Free Methodist Church was established in 1866 with 482 members. In 1871, a small group of Free Methodists including E.P. Hart, the first chairman of the board of trustees, decided to secure 10 acres of land and two buildings in Spring Arbor.

SPRING ARBOR SEMINARY. SAS's May 1873 opening term lacked in many areas: the seminary chapel was not able to hold classes due to a lack of furnishings and the need for repairs. The schoolwork during this semester was rudimentary, so many items were not needed. Eight years later, in 1881, the first class emerged with two graduates: Alice Felt and Lillian Tefft.

The yearbook, first published in 1915 and not again until 1922, manifests a significant lack of images of students, faculty, and campus events. This chapter becomes a faux yearbook for these years by using images and ephemera donated to the SAU Archives. *The Spring Arbor Chronicle*, published from 1897 to 1908, includes "brief notes on campus life and community news."

With the help of a financial agent, SAS maintained a solid financial foundation before its transition to include a junior college. The 1928 graduation included 22 high school and 8 intermediate department graduates. Still applicable today, the SAS semicentennial poem reflects:

> Fifty years have rolled behind us since this school was started out,
> Many times the clouds hung heavy and the devil roared about,
> But our prayers did reach to Heaven and our Father from above
> Gave deliverance from the enemy through His everlasting love.

Elected in 1926, Dr. Merlin G. Smith was the first chief administrator named president rather than principal. Smith also led the school to several major accomplishments, one of which was the transition to a junior college.

SPRING ARBOR SEMINARY AND JUNIOR COLLEGE. Spring Arbor Seminary and Junior College (SASJC) opened on September 3, 1928, offering freshman-year college classes. The decision to offer junior college classes was based on a need for the denomination to offer an opportunity for Free Methodist students who wanted to pursue a Christian education.

In 1930, one of the original campus buildings, the Boys' Dormitory and Chapel, caught fire and collapsed. At the same time, the Great Depression added additional financial burdens to SASJC. Through prayer and fasting, as well as the support of the board of trustees, faculty, staff, teachers, students, and local church members, the school remained open. Howard Snyder sums up this period: "Although junior college work was introduced prior to 1934 and continued until 1963, the twenty-three-year span from 1934–1957 represents the years in which the junior college program was the primary focus of the school—the heyday of the junior college."

As early as 1957, steps were being made to establish a four-year college program.

SPRING ARBOR COLLEGE. The historical and present mission of Spring Arbor College (SAC) is found in its popular Concept, written in 1963. The Concept states that "Spring Arbor College is a community of learners who are distinguished by their serious involvement in the study of the liberal arts, their total commitment to Jesus Christ and their critical participation in the affairs of the contemporary world."

With the Concept as its beacon, SAC added several unique programs. The Christian Perspective in Liberal Arts included the core curriculum and a cross-cultural program so that students come to realize that their perception of others is based on preconceived beliefs and stereotypes, which helps them recognize that everyone is made in God's image. Off-campus programs designed to reach new constituencies included the Prison Education Program.

While continuing its historical mission, Spring Arbor College transitioned to university status. "All the elements of the Concept were threads that ran clear back to 1873 and even before," Snyder wrote, with a change in its wording from Jesus Christ being "a perspective for learning" to "the perspective for learning."

SPRING ARBOR UNIVERSITY. April 30, 2001, marks the celebration day that SAC became Spring Arbor University. Just like its earlier transition from SASJC to SAC, the transition to university status "was made possible and facilitated by the quality of the foundations laid," according to Snyder.

ATHLETICS AT "THE ARBOR." Even though little emphasis was placed on athletics and physical education in the first few decades of the institution's history, athletics became such a significant part of the campus experience and is so well documented that it warrants its own chapter. By the early 1910s, despite the lack of curricular focus, students organized their own athletic activities and tournaments, namely basketball, baseball, and tennis. The school did forbid any playing of football during this time. It was not until the late 1920s that SAS made physical training and athletics a priority in the curriculum under the guise of "treating the body as a temple." Interscholastic athletics were permitted for the first time in 1943. This chapter chronicles some of these early forays into student athletic activity, the growth of varsity sports, development of women's sports, and expansion of the varsity sports teams to a total of 14 as of this writing.

These chapters highlight persons and events using available images. The descriptions for these images used, but are not limited to, the following resources: Snyder's *Concept and Commitment*, school newspapers, alumni publications, and Free Methodist publications. Be aware, transcriptions of photographs may include identification errors at the time of donation.

As for any errors you may find, borrowing from the editors of the 1915 *Academian*, "For all mistakes and omissions we beg your pardon."

One

SETTING THE FOUNDATION

Erected in 1963, the historical marker on campus reads, "Three Michigan institutions of higher education have had their roots here. The predecessor of Albion College, the Spring Arbor Seminary, was chartered in 1835. Michigan Central College, founded in 1844, was located here until its removal in 1855 when it became Hillsdale College. Spring Arbor was opened by Free Methodists in 1873 as an academy with elementary and secondary grades."

Ladies Building Opened in 1846   Chapel Opened in 1848
These Two Buildings, "Ladies Building" and "Chapel," Known as "Michigan Central College" and Located at Spring Arbor, Michigan, were the Starting Point of the Grand Educational Institution now Known as Hillsdale College.

Albion College did not build a school in Spring Arbor. According to Becky Cunningham (1939), a foundation was set near the Kalamazoo River and present-day Sears Road. In 1845, Michigan Central College, founded by the Free-Will Baptists, constructed two buildings on the present-day campus: a chapel with dormitory facilities for boys and a dining facility with a girls' dormitory.

Constructed by Michigan Central College in 1847, this was a boys' dormitory. Around 1873, Moses and Emeline Hart, E.P. Hart's parents, stocked a general store in this building and added living quarters. Buried in Spring Arbor Cemetery, Emeline Stowell Hart died in 1883. After the devastating loss of his wife, Moses, also known as "Father Hart," followed her to await the "resurrection of the just" in 1884.

E.P. and Martha Hart arrived in Michigan pioneering the westward expansion of Free Methodism in 1864. In 1881, the Harts settled in Alameda, California, to continue their evangelistic work. Edward P. Hart, appointed bishop in 1874, resigned in 1908 and died in 1919. He served the Free Methodist Church (FMC) for 46 years. His portrait was painted around the age of seven. (Courtesy of Winston Van Winegarden.)

Gould,   19, Grand Central Block.
                          So. Broadway, Saratoga Springs. N. Y.

The parents of Martha Bishop Hart were identified with the beginnings of the FMC in Marengo, Illinois. After Hart's marriage to Martha, he joined the FMC. Laboring alongside her husband pioneering the FMC, her obituary recalls that "she was always a tower of strength to him and when the books are opened to her will belong much of the glory for the souls won."

The Michigan Conference of the FMC (FMC-MC) was established in 1866. B.T. Roberts presided over the meeting with E.P. Hart as chairman and H.L. Jones, John Ellison, C.S. Gitchell, William Bishop, and L.T. Frink as preachers. The c. 1900 FMC-MC annual meeting is pictured here, held in Addison, Michigan.

Wasson,   ITHACA, MICH.

An early trailblazer in the FMC as well as the FMC-MC, John Ellison ironically attended Hillsdale College for five years studying to be a minister before conversion to Free Methodism by E.P. Hart. Ellison was instrumental in building up circuits where none existed. He lived in Spring Arbor and was an advocate for Spring Arbor Seminary. His niece Alta McConnell attended SAS before marrying the town doctor, Enoch Emerson.

Rev. Chester S. Gitchell, MD, was admitted to the Michigan Conference in 1866 as an inaugural Free Methodist minister and a founding trustee of SAS, working alongside E.P. Hart. Gitchell preached for 53 years beginning in the Illinois Conference. Additionally, beginning in 1893, while preaching only in a local capacity, he practiced medicine, and built up an extensive practice until his death in 1907 at the age of 72. An 1880 autograph book of his daughter Lila, a student at SAS, is in the university archives.

This Gitchell diary entry dated September 25, 1866, reflects the hardship of travel: "I rode all night and this morning at four o'clock the cars stopped at the depot where four of us got off. . . . It is a rainy morning, and as conveyance is here to take us to the place appointed for conference, distance ten miles we started and the rain continued." Five Gitchell diaries dated 1866–1886 are deposited in the SAU archives.

Alongside their evangelical work and expanding the FMC, the Harts raised a family of three daughters: Helen Jones (wife of Bishop Burton R. Jones), Emeline McRae, and Mabel Wolcott. The inscription on the reverse of this image notes the names of the multiple generations: Hart, Jones, MacRae, Wolcott, and Vorheis families. (Courtesy of Winston Van Winegarden.)

Pictured here is Winston Van Winegarden. He and his brother Howard are descendants of two bishops of the FMC. E.P. Hart was their great-grandfather and Bishop Burton R. Jones their grandfather. Winston visited campus in 2008 for the release of Jon S. Kulaga's *Edward Payson Hart: The Second Man of Free Methodism*. (Courtesy of Winston Van Winegarden.)

Bishop Burton R. Jones, widowed two times, married Helen Hart, daughter of E.P. Hart, in 1895. Bishop Jones served the Free Methodist Church in ministry over 52 years including preacher, editor of the FMC publication, teacher at SAS, and bishop from 1894 to 1919. Helen Hart Jones cared for him while he was ill for the last 17 years of his life. Helen, born in 1862 at Marengo, Illinois, died in 1955. She attended SAS at its beginning before moving to California with her father. One daughter was born to this marriage, Ruth J. Winegarden (pictured with her parents). Notable items available for research in the university archives include the 1868 and 1869 diaries of Jones's first wife, Ella; his 1869 and 1918 diaries, the latter chronicling the pandemic; a redwork embroidery quilt from the 1890s; and a late 19th century Hart family photograph album.

The Spring Arbor Methodist Episcopal Church, built in 1854, played an important role for the community. A public meeting established articles of agreement on October 2, 1871, for the establishment of a school. After several years of planning, SAS opened with a shortened term in May 1873.

Two

SPRING ARBOR SEMINARY

A strong emphasis was placed on a sound Christian doctrine for the c. 1882 SAS students. As recorded in the annual conference minutes, "The most perfect religious toleration shall be observed and no student shall be deprived of any of the advantages of [SAS] or be in any manner proscribed while attending the same, on account of his religious convictions and belief." This chapter brings to life the school's early years.

Originally constructed by Michigan Central College, currently known as Hillsdale College, are two frame buildings (left and right) on 10 acres valued at $9,000. The buildings stood unoccupied from 1856 to 1872. In May 1873, twenty-nine elementary and intermediate students attended a first short term. Two high school graduates emerged in 1881, Alice Felt and Lillian M. Tefft. Tefft taught in the Jackson Public Schools for many years.

Clark Jones was the first principal of SAS, serving from 1873 to 1875 and 1877 to 1883. He impressed E.P. Hart by his "all prevailing determination for a higher education." Jones graduated from Albion Commercial College as well as the University of Michigan. He continued to serve in education, both public and private, throughout his lifetime. He died in 1918 and is buried in Spring Arbor Cemetery.

H. Josephine Chittenden (1836–1906), one of the first teachers at SAS, spent 11 and a half years not only educating students' minds but also building up character and cultivating their hearts. Born in Sodus, New York, she desired at a young age to become a teacher. Josephine arrived in Spring Arbor in 1874 with her sister Mary.

Mary Chittenden (1840–1923) intimately knew the spiritual lives of the students and SAS community. She was born in Joy, New York, and was an evangelist for many years in the Free Methodist Church. Her obituary in *The Free Methodist* states that "scattered over our land and in the foreign field are men and women who can point to her home as their spiritual birthplace." In addition to scripture, Chittenden used poetry in counseling students.

The Boys Chapel and Dormitory, built in 1882 and dedicated in 1883, "a large, commodious frame structure, with brick outside," according to *The Free Methodist*, cost approximately $7,500 and "included a first-floor chapel seating up to 400, classroom space, and boys' dormitory." This three-story building became the third building on campus until the original chapel, converted to a music hall, burned down in 1890. (Courtesy of Marston Memorial Historical Center.)

Albert Stilwell served SAS from 1883 to 1893. He was remembered in *The Free Methodist* as "a man white-souled, full-orbed, and strong—a man radiant with the light which gleamed from another world." Stilwell, an ordained minister of the FMC, spent over half a century in some aspect of Christian education. "He did a great work in shaping the lives and destinies of a multitude of students who came under his leadership."

Minnie Luce (1883) is pictured with her husband, W.B. Olmstead, who attended SAS briefly around 1881 while his father pastored in the area. Also pictured are their children (in unknown order) Benjamin, Albert, Raymond, and baby Frances (born 1898). Minnie labored alongside her husband before she became a general missionary and traveled extensively with her husband, the FMC missionary secretary.

Deane Spencer (1891), John Dart (1889), and Florence Harrington Jones (1894) are the only three SAS students identified in this image. Spencer is fifth from left in the sixth row. Dart and Jones are fifth and seventh from left in the fourth row. This is a rare glimpse of SAS students prior to 1889. Spencer and Dart served several Michigan school districts.

Deane Swift Spencer graduated from the University of Michigan with a bachelor of philosophy degree after attending Albion College and was valedictorian of his class in 1897. After working with low-income students, Spencer presented the speech "The Want Wolf" in Detroit. His talk addressed the issue that "children are driven from school to earn money" for family needs, so the government should provide aid for children to become citizens.

The Boy's Dormitory and Chapel, built in 1882 and dedicated by B.T. Roberts in 1883, was the central focus of the small campus. Albert C. Stilwell is possibly pictured here with the SAS students. The enrollment during this time averaged between 98 and 140.

Serving SAS for five years as associate principal, Charles P. Tiffany died from pneumonia at the age of 35. He was remembered in *The Free Methodist* as "an earnest defender of the principles and issues of the church" and "for several years he had charge of the young people's meetings at the seminary, and he took a deep interest in the welfare of the students." He is pictured here with his wife, Jennie, and their daughter.

Prof. Tiffany + family

St. Clear EXTRA FINISH Allen Bennett Block Jackson, Mich

This spring 1890 photograph was taken in front of the Boys' Dormitory, but the event is unknown. Rev. B.T. Roberts dedicated this building in January 1883, preaching on 1 Timothy 6:17–19: "Command those who are rich in this present world not to be arrogant . . . but to put their hope in God . . . so that they may take hold of the life that is truly life."

This 1890s image titled "Spring Arbor Pioneers" pictures, from left to right, (first row) Mrs. Olmstead, unidentified, Sarah Austin, Mrs. Simmonds, Loisa Warner, unidentified, and Edgar Culver; (second row) William Olmstead, Nelson Austin, Jim Bateman, Prof. David Warner, and Catherine Culver. They were residents of Spring Arbor associated with SAS as faculty, their spouses, or parents, as well as local business owners, most notably the meat market.

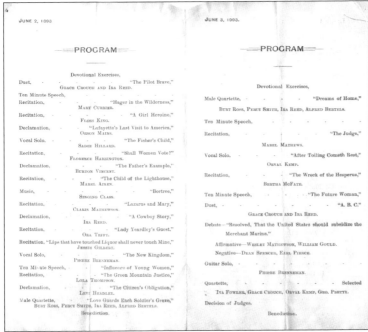

The Alethepian Literary Society was an important feature of school life at the seminary. Meeting weekly, the society was composed of all students, and faculty were considered honorary members. Seeking a high degree of literary culture, contests were held each year in debate and oratory as well as weekly performances including recitations and dialogues.

Howard Snyder relates that the "first twenty years consisted of three years' study on the secondary level" and those students could choose between "the classical, the Latin, or the English" as a "good basic education and prepared them to go on to college if this was their aim." The motto of the junior class of 1894 was "Truth, Purity," and colors were white and gold.

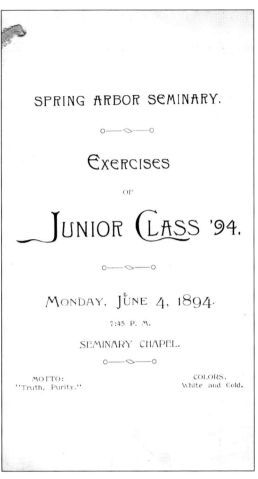

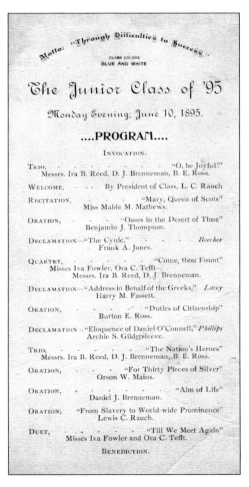

The 1895 program highlights the talents of the SAS students through musical performances, recitations, orations, and declamations. Lewis C. Rauch, class president, presented the welcome as well as an oration titled "From Slavery to World-wide Prominence." In the early 1900s, Lewis was listed as the president of the Business Institute in Detroit.

This is the earliest graduation composite image in the university archives, donated by the descendants of Charles Mains, chairman of the SAS board of trustees from 1885 to 1897. It is also the first graduating class of all men. A gainful farmer in Eckford, Michigan, Mains was also an FMC delegate (1878), supply preacher (1880), and ordained deacon (1884). He moved his family to Spring Arbor, and six of his nine children were enrolled at SAS. The Mains home was on the site of the 1962 library, currently named Dietzman Hall and housing administrative offices. These 1896 graduates are Daniel J. Brenneman, Harry M. Fassett, S. Archie Gildersleeve, Frank A. Jones, Burton S. Mains (middle row, first from left), Orson W. Mains (middle row, second from left), Lewis C. Rauch, Burton E. Ross, and Benjamin J. Thompson.

Born in Canada in 1901 in a home that had its cracks stuffed with rags, Olive Johnson (1923, Alumnus of the Year 1971) dropped out of school at the age of 14. She worked, dreaming of a good education, to help her family of 10. At the age of 19, Johnson enrolled at SAS to finish eighth grade and became its first known African American high school graduate. She is pictured here with other Canadian students. She worked for her room and board in an SAS teacher's home. In her junior year, she obtained employment with a wealthy family in Jackson. This family provided for her expenses to continue her education at Greenville College, where she worked hard to become its first African American graduate. She received a master's degree from the University of Michigan and an honorary doctorate from Greenville College on May 19, 1974. Johnson retired from the Inkster School District in 1967.

Grace Winches Brown (1888) and Belle Winches (1890) were the oldest two children of Andrew Winches, an SAS trustee. Grace attended normal school in Ypsilanti to become a teacher and married Frederick Mains (1888) after the death of her first husband. Belle died in a tragic horse and cart accident on Videto Hill in Spring Arbor after the horse was frightened by a haystack and ran away. Belle taught in the Spring Arbor schools and was on her way to a teachers' convention in Jackson with her sister Grace, who escaped injury. The alumni association lists the graduates of the class of 1888 as Charles Allen, Frederick Mains, and Grace Winches, and 1890 as Grace Hill, Nellie Jones, Wesley Mains, John Roberts, Orrin Tiffany, Ida Tucker, and Belle Winches.

To my Friends —   Always welcome.
My Album is a garden spot
Where all my friends may sow
Where thorns and thistles flourish not
But flowers alone may grow
With smiles for sunshine tears
    for showers
I'll water watch and guard my
    flowers

Gracie Simmonds

The autograph book of Grace Simmonds (1900) donated to the university archives is a precious reminder of the students attending the seminary at the turn of the 20th century. Several generations of descendants of Grace Simmonds followed in her footsteps, including Janice Snyder, the wife of SAU historian Howard A. Snyder.

The alumni association lists the graduates of 1902 as Nathan J. Aikin, Charles E. Caswell, Myrtle B. Crouch, Rolland E. Crouch, Myrtle L. Jones, Elba L. Morse, M. Belle Roberts, and Grace E. Smith. The principal, pictured at center, was Rev. David S. Warner. The enrollment of SAS reached 70 this term. On September 19, 1901, school exercises were cancelled and a memorial service was held for President McKinley.

Jennie Walls was the valedictorian and only graduate in her class of 1903. Sent by her aunt after the death of her parents, Walls attended SAS to become a teacher. After graduation, she taught at SAS until December 1905. Her graduation gown was found, as well as a copy of her valedictory address, "The Ministry of Difficulties." Walls married Henry Hamilton in 1905 and shared a "lifetime ministry of pastoring, evangelism, and Free Methodist church planting" in Canada, according to *The Free Methodist*, while raising 11 children. The photograph below was taken after the death of her mother, who was superimposed into the family portrait. Valerie Trexler, granddaughter of Jennie Walls Hamilton and wife of retired SAU professor Fred Trexler, donated Jennie's graduation gown and graduation artifacts to the archives.

The Administration Hall building, dedicated on June 11, 1905, was described in The *Spring Arbor Chronicle* as "48x65 feet and two stories high, with a basement full size and a large room under the roof" and "housed classrooms, the principal's office, a library, two music rooms, a cloak room, and a chapel room." The *Chronicle* also wrote that "The building is wired for electrical bell service, which will be connected with the boys' dormitory and boarding hall. With this in commission, the classes will be called, which will do away with the ringing of the chapel bell for class calls." The chapel was named after Carrie Turrell Burritt, "who contributed liberally toward the erection of the building," and designated in gold letters over the doorway "Burritt Chapel." Sister Burritt taught in public school until her marriage to Eldon Grant Burritt—president of Greenville College in 1908—and was general president of the Women's Missionary Society of the Free Methodist Church from 1927 to 1939.

Born to Free Methodist minister P.E. Vincent in 1877 and named after Michigan FMC pioneer B.R. Jones, Burton J. Vincent (1895) served as principal of SAS from 1905 to 1909 after attending Marion College, then completing a correspondence course for his degree. Vincent later became a bishop in the FMC known as "an unusual leader of young people," according to *The Free Methodist*. (Courtesy of Marston Memorial Historical Center.)

This image is labeled "1905." Zella Emerson (1914), the girl with the bowtie at center, lists, but does not identify, the following students in her scrapbook: Hazel Rauch, Emma Miller, Percy Reed, Hattie Page, Nora (?), Fred Timbers, Joy Rauch (1916), Harold (?), Walter Reed (1914), Mabel Peters, and Marjorie Peters.

Eulalia Snyder Buttelman (1906) became a teacher of music at SAS in 1907 and was described in the *Journal* as "a young lady who has rare talent in the line of music [with] native musical talent." The *Journal* also reported that Snyder married her husband, Clifford, in 1913 and "became accompanist for many internationally known [opera] artists" as well as gaining "acclaim for creating opera miniatures and operalogues."

The alumni association lists the graduates of 1906 as Alice Arnold (second row, third from left), Alice Asplin, Lela Backus, Charles Collins (first row, first from left), Elsie Collins (second row, second from left), William Cross (top row, third from left), Burton A. Hartle, Anna Irwin, Trevor Muffitt, Artley Newell, Eulalia Snyder, Mabel Stowell, Albert Tate, and John Timbers.

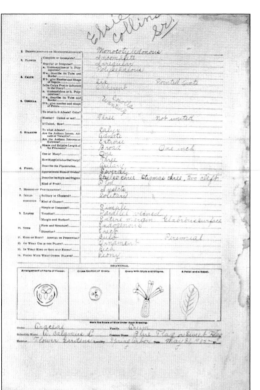

A botany field book dating to 1906 titled *Herbarium and Plant Analysis* contains 35 plant specimens from the Spring Arbor area. It belonged to Elsie Irene Collins (1906) and was donated to the archives by her great-nephew Walter Rosser. According to Rosser, Collins taught school after graduation in Kansas and "every summer she would return home, bringing her piano on the train." She continued to teach until her retirement in 1947.

Donated by the family of Burton Ashley Hartle (1906), this embroidered, autographed handkerchief is labeled "Winter Term '05." It contains many signatures of the SAS students and community. *The Spring Arbor Chronicle* reported that "there are now 60 in the school family. Warren Woodworth, who is now at the hall, finds that he must cook a large amount of food to satisfy the hunger of that number."

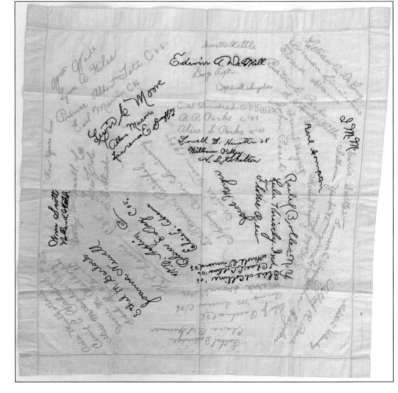

The alumni association lists the class of 1907 as Harvey Dawson, L. Glenn Lewis, Grace Waldorph, and Loyal C. Watters. *The Spring Arbor Chronicle* reports that for approximately $115 tuition and board, in 1907, rooms were "furnished with bed, mattress and springs, study table, commode, washbowl and pitcher, looking-glass and chairs," along with lamps and oil and a steam radiator. However, students were asked to bring their own carpet.

"The Faculty Twins," Eulalia Snyder (Music Department) and Aimee W. King (Primary Department), are pictured in October 1907. The alumni association lists the class of 1908 as Flossie Barr, Florus Broomfield, Mrs. H.D. Gorby, Arthur Miller, Asenath J. Montgomery, R. Carroll Olmstead, Grace M. Rawson, Edgar Thompson, Rolland Welch, and Charles C. Whistler.

Ida Gage (No. 62)—a prolific Free Methodist licensed conference evangelist, architect of many FM church plans across Ohio, and a strong advocate for woman ordination—served as matron of women at SAS around 1907. Her grandson Glenn V. Tingley, a famous Christian and Missionary Alliance minister, lived with her while his father attended SAS. Gage's biographical information was provided by Christy Mesaros-Winckles (2005, 2008).

Rolland Welch (1908) and his wife, Lottie, served as missionaries to China from 1917 to 1923. Rolland, a medical missionary, and Lottie returned from China in 1924. Until his death in 1934, Rolland practiced medicine in Bellevue, Michigan. This image is labelled as the 1908 or 1909 senior banquet. (Courtesy of Marston Memorial Historical Center.)

The alumni association lists the class of 1909 as Ina A. Cusick, Charles H. DeLong, Eathel V. Dodridge, Lena P. Duell, Alice E. Evans, Lowell S. Hunter, Harry D. Gorby, Saxton Jacobs, Kate P. Leininger, Victor E. Rensberry, Hazel J. Schwarzentraub, J. Frank Smith, and Mildred E. Stone. B.J. Vincent (center) was principal.

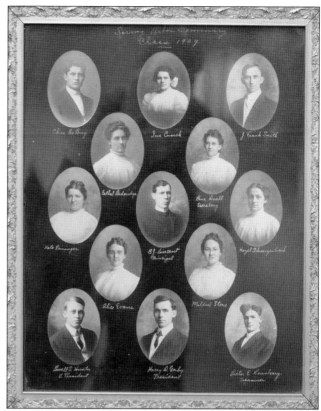

This photograph, identified as "1909 students with Vincents," could show the class of 1910. The alumni association lists the 1910 class members as George R. Backus, Katherine C. Bassett, Ruth F. Hitt, Harold H. Hunter, Howard L. Kingsley, Lynn A. Niles, Edwin P. Reed, and Harry Schwarzentraub.

Images of the interiors of buildings on the SAS campus are very rare. This is a c. 1922 photograph taken inside a dorm room donated by Diane Kurtz (1973, 2007 Leroy M. Lowell Award), wife of Dan Kurtz (1974), granddaughter of Rena Hebberd Hyndman (1922) and Howard Hyndman (1923).

Seen in this image, the alumni association lists the class of 1911 as Harry B. Anstead, Mary L. Aseltine, Reuben J. Baker, George H. Coleman, Mabel P. Cowell, Fred E. Dodds, S. Hubert Doering, Bertha Fader Messeroll, Marion A. Tharpe, David M. Wells, Eunice M. White, and Lucy E. Wilkinson.

The alumni association lists the class of 1912 as Floyd J. Connor, Lawrence E. Connor, Sherman T. Cross, Ottie B. Dawson, Leah M. Ewing, Mattie Kenworthy, Alice M. Knapp, H. Eison Leininger, Ruth I. McFate, Mabel Peters, Floyd A. Putter, J. Fred Qulg, James Trickey, and Margaret Bailey Wells.

This postcard shows the ladies' student picnic on Halloween around 1911 in the front of campus, near the old post office. Ruth, "standing on her toes to be the tallest," sent it to R.C. Campbell in Ann Arbor. At far right is Bertha Fader Messeroll (1911). She became a member of the SAS faculty in 1913 after attending Ypsilanti State Normal School and remained in the SAS Intermediate Department until 1924.

39

This photograph is labeled "Intermediates—Teacher Asenath Montgomery (2nd right)—about 1912." Perhaps Montgomery (1908) taught at SAS for a few years before attending Greenville College and receiving her bachelor of pedagogy in 1914. She was one of three daughters and four sons born to Rev. Hiram Montgomery, whose ministry brought the family to Spring Arbor for a short time. Reverend Montgomery served the FMC for over 40 years until his departure in 1929 "with the harness on," according to *The Free Methodist*.

The alumni association lists the class of 1913 as Francis Barnes, W. McKinley Bates, Clara M. Cross, Irene Doering, Thomas Z. Hadley, Ruth I. Kentworthy, Harriet Lee, Frank Palmer, St. Clair Pardee, Mark B. Rauch, Eunice Ross, and Grace Somerville.

Harriet Mae Lee (1913) married John Malmsberry in 1915. The marriage certificate lists her residence as Ohio and occupation in 1915 as schoolteacher. It was reported by *The Free Methodist* that the class of 1913, by its "marked ability evidenced by them in the closing exercises for the year speak in loudest terms of praise for the teaching force and educational methods" at SAS.

"My grandmother, Myrl Parsons, third from right" is handwritten on the reverse of this 1912–1913 faculty photograph. Pictured in unknown order are Maude Stewart, Mrs. Howard, Ethel Damon, Bertha Fader Messeroll (1911), Miss Buel, Ruth Avery, Prof. J. Arthur Howard, Prof. Henry Stewart, and Rev. John Timbers (1906). Timbers graduated in 1906, along with 11 others, noted to be a representative class of strong characters. Timbers delivered an oration titled "The Object of Life."

"My grandmother, Myrl Parsons, second from left" is handwritten on the reverse of this undated faculty photograph. The 1915 *Academian* lists her as the music director, receiving a master's degree from the Weltner Conservatory of Music in St. Louis, Missouri, where she studied under a pupil of the world-renowned Ferruccio Busoni. Parsons is known to have taken much pleasure in her students.

Zella Emerson Gilmore (1914) was the daughter of Dr. Enoch Emerson and Alta McConnell Emerson. Dr. Enoch Emerson, the local Spring Arbor physician, married Alta McConnell, the niece of John Ellison, a pioneer Free Methodist minister as well as founding board member of SAS. Zella Gilmore is pictured here in 1914.

Zella Emerson Gilmore's mother, Alta McConnell, attended SAS in the late 1870s. Zella's granddaughter Judy Pfaff donated Gilmore's SAS scrapbook documenting her primary and secondary school years at SAS. Included in this collection are items dated to the late 1800s. This image of early student life is from her scrapbook.

Zella Emerson Gilmore remained at SAS for an additional year before attending normal school. The governor officially praised her for teaching over 50 years in the state of Michigan, including second and third generations of children. The Hanover Museum named a c. 1900 classroom in her honor. This postcard of early Spring Arbor Township shows the view looking west down Main Street from campus.

This postcard, postmarked September 29, 1914, reads: "Dear Ma. This is a train wreck that happened at Spring Arbor station. This is the engine and there was 16 cars burning in a pile back of the engine the cars was full of pig and one of meat butter and eggs. One man killed we had no school that day and all went to see it." (Courtesy of Bob Pohl.)

The alumni association lists the class of 1914 as Charlotte Bailey, Maude Cassidy, Charles Dornton, Zella Emerson, Marjory Goodhew, Frank Lee, Ralph Lee, Mildred Marshall, Marjorie Meek, Walter Reed, Lynn Scofield, Samuel Kannel, Leon Voorheis, and Hugh Vore. This picture shows unidentified intermediate students in 1914.

REPORT CARD
SPRING ARBOR SEMINARY

Term Ending _Jan 2 3_ 191_4_

		EXAMINAT'N	RECORD
1	Bible Study	93	96
2	Virgil		94
3	Zoology		93
4	English IV		96.
5	Physics		$94\frac{1}{3}$
6			

_____ Principal

This 1914 student's report card reflects classes taken in the final term before high school graduation from SAS. Earlier studies, in addition to mathematics and language arts, were algebra, ancient history, Caesar, Caesar and prose, Cicero, German, geometry, Latin, and penmanship. The report card collection in the university archives spans over a decade from 1902 to 1914.

The first yearbook, *Academian*, was "to give the outside world a view of our school life and ideal" and to "build up this school, whose purpose is to unite the true and never changing standard of God's salvation with the intellectual training of the mind." Pictured here is Zella Emerson Gilmore and members of the editorial staff of the *Academian*. The next yearbook would not be published until 1922.

In 1909, Leon D. Voorheis (1914) enrolled in SAS at the age of 19 after recovering from a heart attack while attending public school. He continued his education at SAS after graduation to prepare for the ministry. He is pictured here with his wife, Ruth McFate (1912), son Eldon, and daughter Janet (high school 1948, junior college 1950), wife of SAC's first president, David McKenna (1949).

The alumni association lists the class of 1916 as Helen Aldrich, Mark Bigelow, Cora Dennis, Cora Dodds, Bertha Dodds, Esther Green, Lucile Green, Bertha Hartle, Lillian Houghtby, Mildred Marshall, Ada Mudford, Ruth Mudford, Joy Rauch, Eli Richard, Howard Tefft, Fred Timbers, and Florence Woodard.

William V. Miller served as principal of SAS between 1924 and 1926. He is pictured in this 1916 SAS faculty and staff portrait. From left to right are (first row) Bertha Fader (1911), Mrs. Miller, Bessie Leitle (cook), Maude Stewart, Miss Kaiser, and Marjory Goodhew (1914); (second row) Persis Phelps (English), W.V. Miller (Bible, Latin), Henry Stewart (principal), Martha Montgomery, and Rose Kinney (cook).

Henry Stewart (pictured here), principal of SAS from 1912 to 1917 and 1920 to 1924, is described by Snyder as "perhaps the first to clearly articulate the view that Christian belief is not merely something tacked on to secular education, but that all real truth—and therefore all true education—begins with the Truth revealed in Jesus Christ and the Bible."

David S. Warner, fifth from left in back in this image labeled "1918 Board of Trustees," served SAS for 49 years up until his death. His service included teacher, principal, member of the board of trustees, and president for many years. His obituary in *The Free Methodist* noted that "without his friendship and interest SAS could not have influenced the world for good as it has done."

The 1920 SAS Board of Trustees is, from left to right, (first row) Prof. Henry Stewart, principal; W.J. Jackson; W.C. Muffitt; Frank Houghtby; Hiram Porterfield; and Frank L. Baker; (second row) H. DeForrest Gaffin; D.W. Wesley; George Peters; Walter A. Sayre; Peter White; Bishop David S. Warner; and John Timbers.

This class of 1920 group photograph includes the married names of "the class I took through high school," as inscribed on the reverse. From left to right are (first row) Grace Vore (Demeray), Mary King (Kenworthy), Nellie Lillard, Margaret Crucius, unidentified, and Beulah Carr (Morton); (second row) Edna Baker (Agnew), Paul Kenworthy, Bertha Fader (Messeroll) (honorary member), Earl Fletcher, and Jessie Ragatz (Booth).

Alice M. Barber (1899) "graced every office to which the church appointed her," according to the *Bulletin*. She taught during the SAS 1925–1926 school year, roomed over 50 students, and was a "Class Leader of students groups," according to her obituary in the *Bulletin*, and "a faithful letter writer and prayer partner to many missionaries." She is pictured here with her brother Walter in Spring Arbor.

In 1920, at the age of 19, Hugh A. White (1923) entered SAS. His delayed entry into high school was necessary because while he was in the eighth grade, his father suffered a heart attack, causing White to temporarily take over the responsibility of the farm. During his time here, his leadership abilities were recognized as he was the president of the senior class and business manager of the yearbook as well as president of the athletic association. After completing his high school degree in three years, White continued his education and received his master's in business education and became a certified public accountant in 1931. In 1933, White joined the board of trustees and helped to financially stabilize the institution. He remembered that during those days, "you couldn't drive it in an hour and ten minutes because you had poor roads and there were no superhighways" to attend the many board meetings held in Spring Arbor. In his professional life, White was a founder and managing partner of an accounting firm.

Hugh A. White's footprints, left all over the world as a missionary traveler, are most significant as chairman of the board of trustees. Not only did he financially stabilize SAS during the Depression, the White family contributed to Lowell Hall and the 1963 library. He is honored as "the man whose courage and vision have rewritten the modern history of Spring Arbor College." The 2002 library building is named the Hugh A. and Edna C. White Library. Pictured here are White being honored with an honorary doctorate and as Distinguished Alumnus of the Year in 1967 and his wife, Edna, who served tirelessly alongside him. The White legacy continues to this day through the White Foundation. Family members have also served in various roles, including son Glenn White as chairman of the board, grandson Charles as faculty member, and grandson David (1973) as board of trustees member. Recently, a notice of sale of SAS published by a creditor in 1935 in a local newspaper was discovered. It documents family history that Hugh White had taken a grocer's debt into his name to avoid the sale of the school.

James G. Fortress died on June 8, 1977, at the age of 97 in Jackson, Michigan. According to his obituary in *Light & Life*, "He was ordained in 1950 by Bishop E.P. Hart. He had heard all the bishops preach, except one. It is believed that he was the last living person to have heard B.T. Roberts preach. He dearly loved the Free Methodist Church. It was during his pastorate in Spring Arbor in 1923 that the original stone church was built [pictured below]. The memorial service was conducted in the Spring Arbor Church by John E. Hendricks, whom he considered one of the great preachers in the history of Free Methodism, and Robert A. Maxwell who especially befriended him in his declining years. His esteemed superintendent, Frank Van Valin, sang his favorite hymn."

Three

SPRING ARBOR SEMINARY AND JUNIOR COLLEGE

The c. 1958 signs erected near the east and west boundaries of the village served a threefold purpose: to announce the village, name the campus, and testify to the major purpose of Spring Arbor Junior College (SAJC) and High School (SAHS) as "Christ-Centered Education." The opportunity to take first-year junior college classes began in 1923, and second-year classes were added in 1929.

This is one of a few cemetery photographs, usually showing a female student sitting atop a gravestone, an unofficial Spring Arbor pastime. Here, Thelma Rickard (1929, 1931) sits on the gravestone of Rev. Birney Alberts. According to *The Free Methodist*, Alberts spent his "final years on the Seminary faculty in the Bible and Theological Department." Rickard returned to campus as a bookkeeper in the 1940s.

On December 6, 1930, as reported in the *Bulletin*, "a fire of unknown origin reduced to ashes and debris the old brick dormitory and chapel," starting in the attic at 3:45 p.m. The "earnest" young resident men lost most everything by 5:30 p.m. "Providentially the roofs and leaves were soaked from recent rains" and "the winds blew the fire away from the other buildings."

In addition to chapel fire photographs, a scrapbook donated by Shannon Hoover (1932) also contains this image of Roland Sayre (1932) in front of the "frat house." Spring Arbor Seminary viewed fraternities as preparatory to membership in "oath-bound secret orders," and none existed on campus. In 1931, the "frat" boys moved to the Hilliard House.

An auditorium–gymnasium, built in 1931, was dedicated as the Merlin G. Smith Gymnasium in 1950. The building measured 50 by 100 feet with a seating capacity of 1,000. In 1950, it underwent a complete modernization. It was renovated in 1991 to house the music department and renamed the Smith Music Center. Dr. Merlin G. Smith served as president from 1926 to 1934 before becoming president at Roberts Wesleyan College.

Charles Kingsley (1928, 1931) was the son of William D. Kingsley Jr. (1904) and grandson of Free Methodist minister W.D. Kingsley, who was ordained in 1898. Charles Kingsley became director of public relations and taught classes at the junior college before becoming the first fulltime director of the Light and Life Men's Fellowship. Charles continued his service on the Spring Arbor board of trustees for 27 years and was 1972 Alumnus of the Year. He is pictured below with his nephew Charles (1992), brother of Rob Kingsley, assistant registrar of global undergraduate at Spring Arbor University from 1988 to 2023. Four generations of Kingsleys attended SAU, including Rob and Charles's father, Virgil Kingsley (1939, 1941); Lillian (1933, 1935); George (1937); Barbara (1967); Beth (1961); Burton (1961); Janet (1968); Joyce (1971); and Joanne (1974).

On May 17, 1931, the newspaper headlines read that a "Class of 87 to Be Graduated June 2 May be Last Unless Financial Campaign, Starting Today Is Successful in Raising Fund of $125,000." According to Snyder's history, the Great Depression was a time of crisis for Spring Arbor. "Walker and Ruth Towns recalled, 'Faculty members took part of their salaries by getting what groceries were available at the school store. The remainder of the salaries were unpaid for months.' Some faculty took odd jobs on Saturdays during summers. Walker Towns earned 35¢ an hour working at Beuhler's Meat Market each Saturday and 'worked in the hay field in the summer to pay for milk.' " Pictured are Prof. Walker and Ruth Towns with their children Ronald and Robart. In 1932, the board of trustees cut the faculty salaries by 25 percent and recommitted to "continue the historic commitment to quality liberal arts education for all Free Methodist young people," and with the help of Hugh A. White and the Spring Arbor League, this financial crisis passed.

Clarence D. Decan served as business manager from 1934 until his retirement in 1949. The *Bulletin* praised him for his "strenuous service . . . the never tiring efforts of this man and his helpers." Four buildings were constructed on campus under his guidance. Decan then became the superintendent of construction for home missions for the Free Methodist Church.

On February 19, 1939, a new science-chapel building was dedicated by Bishop Mark D. Ormston to be known as Decan Hall. Two science labs, a chapel, and a college study hall were provided by the addition of this campus building, allowing a second story to be added when funds become available. Dr. David McKenna (1949), working alongside Clarence Decan, remembers "the steady hand that worked construction miracles with the most unskilled crew."

Beverly E. Cunningham's (1939) love for the preservation of the history of Spring Arbor is evident through her many projects. After graduating from SAHS, she obtained her registered nursing degree and was also the Spring Arbor postmaster. She published several books, including the history of Spring Arbor and Falling Waters Park, as well as lining the Falling Waters Trail with historical markers. On campus, she designed and funded the campus corridor relating early school history. Cunningham is pictured above with Richard Zeller (1938) at the dedication of the Snyder School House. Her research files are housed in the local history research room in the White Library and funded by Cunningham.

According to Wanda Schulcz (1959, 1961), her father moved to Spring Arbor as a foreman for Spring Arbor College Industries after being recruited by Free Methodist minister Rev. Warner R. Parks, who provided employment to students by making pallets to supplement their income. This c. 1940s image shows Spring Arbor College Industries, which is now Jaworski Nursing Labs.

Dedicated on September 4, 1944, this honor roll of World War II veterans was built on the southwest corner of campus at College Street and M60. During the years 1943–1945, the *News on Parade* publication was a monthly paper to keep servicemen abreast of news from home.

Built to replace the century-old, antiquated dormitory, a new dormitory housing 70 girls opened in October 1941 and was dedicated in 1942 to Rev. and Mrs. W.C. Muffitt, lifelong friends of the school. At dedication, the *Bulletin* wrote, "Brother Muffitt has been a member of the Board of Trustees since 1897 . . . through their assistance, many young people who would otherwise have been denied an education have been trained for places of usefulness." In 2019, Muffitt Hall was demolished to make additional green space on the plaza. Pictured below from left to right are Bishop Ormston, Rev. W.C. Muffitt, Edna Muffitt, and unidentified.

Lawrence W. Hester attended the junior college only one year, his freshman year of 1942–1943, before he volunteered for the Navy. Hester donated his remarkable scrapbook documenting his year at SAJC to the archives so that it may "return to its ancestral home." Pictured here is Hester "going to Mr. Moon's Physical Geography Class."

Among the subjects Lawrence Hester documented in his scrapbook are Campus Day 1942, couples on campus, buildings, "Spring Arbor's Manpower Shortage Ratio: 5 girls to 1 boy," "Hossie" as "Spring Arbor's Glamour Girl," students, and faculty. Hester labeled this image "The H.S. class of '42' paints the Senior Rock" and noted that they were "Busy as a Bee."

Arleta Richardson (1944, Alumnus of the Year 1996) received her bachelor of science degree from Western Michigan University then returned to SAJC as a teacher and librarian until 1953 before relocating to Los Angeles. She published the first book in the popular Grandma's Attic series in 1974. In the years following, she wrote over 30 children's books and other publications that have been translated into several languages. Other accomplishments include World War II service, director of missions education for the Free Methodist Women's Missionary Society, and a book tour in Japan. Her books and writings continue to be celebrated and cherished today. The image below from her scrapbook is labeled "Skip Hike–44, All the class but Betty and Bob."

Completed in 1946, the Maycroft Administration Hall was used to house veterans until 1947. It is in the center block of campus, built over the campus steam heating plant approximately five feet above ground. An addition in 1959 added new offices at ground level. A name change to the Munger Administration Building occurred in the 1960s.

Once known as the Hall of Science, the second floor added to Decan Hall was being used for classes in February 1948. At this time, a pilot's license course was added to the curriculum, and the 75th spring commencement was being planned for 90 students in the high school and junior college departments.

SPRING ARBOR JUNIOR COLLEGE
BOY'S DORMITORY

Built in 1947, Ormston Hall for men housed 90 students and was named for Bishop Mark D. Ormston. Beginning his ministry in 1916, "he gave to the church more than 40 years of active service," according to *The Free Methodist*, served on the board of trustees, including as president, and "played a big part in establishing the campus facilities which we now have." Ormston's daughter Grace (1939, 1941) attended SAHS and SAJC, as did his grandson Dale Stephenson (1979), who recently served in the same role as his grandfather as chairman of the board of trustees. Robbie Bolton (1998), Ormston Hall resident director from 2002 to 2008, states that "Ormston was a unique community of men hosting campus events i.e. Porchfest and a live nativity. There were also midnight forays into the tunnels under the campus." A collection of Ormston men's annual photographs from 1988 to 2018 is digitized and available for research. This building is undergoing renovations to house administrative offices.

Field service began in the fall of 1948. Gospel teams were comprised of "a student preacher and singers" that "held many services, several in churches other than Free Methodist," according to the *Bulletin*. In the first semester, the Field Service Department performed at over 200 services. Pictured here are some members of the 1951 field service teams: Crusader's Quartet, Harmony Trio, King's Herald, Jubilairs, Triumphant Trio, and Banner Quartet. Charles Kingsley, director of the Field Service Department, is standing at left. His yearbook description reads that "he has no parallel—he is humor and seriousness and Field Service in one package." Floyd McCallum, the religion, philosophy, and Greek professor, is standing at right. The yearbook described him as "a true genius in the classroom; in the pulpit. When he opens his mouth something original and unique is sure to flow forth."

The E.P. Hart Memorial Chapel was dedicated on May 5, 1951, by Bishop Ormston. After the chapel fire in 1930, there was no dedicated chapel building for two decades, and services were held in Decan Hall. This facility seated 1,000 people with a spacious platform and curtains for performances. The chapel was renovated in 1999 through the generosity of Glenn and Ruth White.

Memorial Classroom Hall, dedicated on January 16, 1954, connected E.P. Hart Memorial Chapel and Decan Hall. Eight classrooms, a counseling office, and a faculty lounge were welcome additions to campus. The *Bulletin* announced: "This memorial to the Christian Teacher . . . will complete the academic section of the front of the campus" to replace the defunct administration building.

This 1947 aerial view of campus, when "seminary" was removed from the school name, was taken during the construction of Ormston Hall. In the background, notice "Vetville," single-story housing for World War II veterans. In 1958, the board of trustees authorized "the immediate start of plans to enter the field as a four-year liberal arts college" with junior-year college classes starting in the fall of 1962. A decade of progress from the time of this photograph until 1958 included E.P. Hart Memorial Chapel, Sayre Hall, Post House, and the shop and home economics building. Under the direction of Pres. Roderick J. Smith and the newly initiated developmental council, a new plan titled "Decade of Development" included a high school men's dormitory, student center, and fieldhouse. For this decade of development, the estimated cost of all the buildings and improvements was $1.3 million, and the plan promised that "SAJC's greatest days lie ahead."

Four

SPRING ARBOR COLLEGE

The men of Ormston I pose for their floor photograph on the roof of the Spring Arbor Free Methodist Church during the 1986–1987 school year. During the Spring Arbor College years, where students lived on campus was often a significant source of pride and identity. Future iterations of the student handbook would specifically prohibit being on the roof of campus buildings.

Every September since 1984, students have participated in the tradition of Arbor Games, which pits residence halls against each other. Activities include skit competitions, tug of war, egg toss, and bat spin, to name a few. Each Arbor Games begins with a ceremony in which a torch is lit by a member of the faculty or staff adorned in a toga and a crown of laurels.

Arbor Games began as the brainchild of Barb Wagner (1986). Pictured here is Pres. Kenneth Coffman in the Spring Arbor College sweatshirt adjudicating a tug of war contest during the 1987 Arbor Games. Coffman was enthusiastically involved in the first few years of Arbor Games. The competition has been held every year since 1984 except for 2020 due to the COVID-19 pandemic.

For many years, Roger Varland, professor of art and history, was the master of ceremonies for Arbor Games. He is pictured here providing direction to the Arbor Games masses. Varland served on the faculty from 1985 to 2016. Prior to joining the faculty, he served as the resident director of Ormston Hall. He is credited with creating the 40-plus year tradition of Ormston Porchfest.

According to Roger Varland, Ormston Porchfest began with a group of students screening the film *Chariots of Fire* on the porch of Ormston Hall in 1982. The following year, the event was repeated with students running around the building dressed as *Chariots of Fire* characters. It is not just an event for students—faculty like Mary Darling (1978) and Carla Koontz (right) were a frequent presence at Porchfest.

Over the years, Porchfest became a school-year-ending event including cover bands, videos, and comedy sketches often culminating in a performance by Ormston men performing "So Long Farewell" from *The Sound of Music*. Originally held on the Ormston porch, the event was later moved to the Ogle Dining Commons and then to the Dunckel Gymnasium. Pictured here is a student group performing on the Ormston porch in the early 1990s.

Free hot dogs were a staple of most Ormston Porchfests. What began as a buffet line eventually devolved into years of heaving hot dogs into the crowd. Pictured here "distributing" hot dogs from under his sombrero is former Ormston Hall resident director and associate dean of students Bobby Pratt (1992, 2008, 2017 Leroy M. Lowell Award).

In the Western High School gymnasium on December 2, 1961, SAC crowned its first homecoming queen. Carolyn Lietzke (1962) was congratulated by Pres. David McKenna (1949). The queen was escorted by student association president Burton Jones (1962). In this photograph, Lietzke is joined by members of the homecoming court. From left to right are Norma Kelly (1962), Joyce Kingsbury (1961, 1966), Estelle Yates (1962), and Karen Rust (1962).

Leslie Dietzman (1962) served on the board of trustees for over 30 years, including as board chairman. He received the Alumni Young Leader Award in 1979 and was named Alumnus of the Year in 2000. Once the library moved to its new building, the old library building was renovated and rededicated as Dietzman Hall in appreciation of him and his wife Estelle's (1962) contributions to Spring Arbor University.

Days before the 1992 election, Vice Pres. Dan Quayle visited SAC to host a rally as part of Pres. George H.W. Bush's re-election campaign. Quayle (left) is on stage alongside SAC president Allen Carden. In the background is Michigan governor John Engler. Throughout its history, SAC has brought thinkers and politicians to engage with students. In 2015, presidential candidate Ben Carson hosted a rally at SAU at the invitation of Pres. Brent Ellis.

SAU has always engaged with diverse viewpoints on contemporary issues. In March 1993, SAC hosted an event titled "Ethical Alternatives to Assisted Suicide" with guest speaker attorney Geoffrey Feiger. Feiger was the legal representation for the infamous assisted suicide doctor Jack Kevorkian. A few years later, in 1998, Feiger unsuccessfully ran as the Democratic nominee for governor of Michigan.

There have been many musical performance groups over the years, from the more traditional concert, jazz, and pep bands and chamber, concert, and festival choirs to the less formal groups like Asland, Agape Singers, New Dawn, and Morning Praise, to name a few. Pictured here is the 1977–1978 SAC jazz band under the direction of Kennistan Bauman posing for a group photograph in front of Centennial Gardens. From left to right are (first row) Gale Hurst (1978); (second row) Gordy Iocco (1981), Brad Kennedy (1980), Lori Ormston (1980), Keith Burk (1981), Theresa Wilson (1979), Dan Stevens (1983), and John Blewett (1981); (third row) Sindy Jacobus (1980), Dale Stephenson (1979), John Finley (1979), Doug Sanford (1978), Brian Hazard (1979), Brian Mielke (1981), Janell Farris (1979), Brent Smith (1979), Ken Mills (1978), Duane Skene (1978), Brad Lockwood (1978), Kevin Newcomber (1980), and director Ken Bauman. Bauman joined the faculty in 1970 and spent the next 25 years growing an active band program. He was recognized in 1996 with the Leroy M. Lowell award for excellence in employee service.

Joseph Jaworski (1972) spent over 36 years sharing his love of plants, fishing, and people with his Spring Arbor students as a professor of biology. He was so committed to the sciences at SAU that, after he passed away in 2015, his estate funded the Jaworski Clinical Simulation Center.

Jaworski was eccentric, funny, and innovative in his teaching style. Former student Maria Crawford (2004) fondly recalls many fun learning activities in his class, including making homemade root beer. His biology colleague Chris Newhouse noted that he was dedicated "to the spiritual and educational development of students." Given his love of plants, it is fitting that a tree was planted in his honor in front of the Whiteman-Gibbs Science Center.

The 1940s aerial view of campus below shows the location of the exalted oak tree between the Kresge Student Center and Lowell Hall. According to Larry Ousley, longtime facilities director, the oak tree is over 250 years old and was growing during Colonial times. The oak tree has hosted many campus gatherings over the years from freshman partings to Lowell Luaus. The Dorrice A. Ogle Dining Commons renovation in 2013 included a wall of windows affording maximum visibility of the magnificent oak. So inspiring is this great oak that English professor Brent Cline (2020) and library director Robbie Bolton (1998) championed replacing the cougar mascot with "Fightin' Oaks." Pres. Brent Ellis once reflected, "As I observe the majesty of the oak, I am reminded of the abiding presence of our Lord throughout our history. As the oak remains, so does our Lord."

On the eve of final exams, faculty and staff serve a late-night meal while holiday-themed skits are performed and carols are sung. Serving in the kitchen at the 1992 Midnight Breakfast are Assistant Vice President for College Relations Sharon Pitts (1991, left) and Denice Carden (right), wife of Pres. Allen Carden, who served from 1991 to 1996.

Glenn White served on the board of trustees for 39 years, including 20 years as chairman of the board. When the E.P. Hart Memorial Chapel needed significant renovations, Glenn and his wife, Ruth, generously provided the support, and it was renamed the Glenn and Ruth White Auditorium in their honor. All three of their children attended SAU: Charles, David (1973), and Nancy (1974).

As construction of the Centennial Gardens goes on around him, Pres. Elwood Voller (left) holds up a miniature sculpture of a lamp, cross, and world for George N. Higgins (center) and Hugh White (1923, right). In 1973, the Centennial Gardens were built to celebrate the first 100 years of SAC. The fountain sculpture was designed by James J. Snyder (1948, 1958). The lamp, cross, and world, which incorporated SAC's logo at the time, were meant to symbolize the SAC mission statement, the Concept. This sculpture would inform the new SAU logo when it was redesigned to coincide with achieving university status in 2001. In recent years, students have affectionately referred to this statue in the Centennial Gardens as the "Jesus Reactor" because of the atom-like appearance around the cross.

THE CENTENNIAL GARDENS
May 18, 1974
Constructed during the College's 100th anniversary year to commemorate a century of service as a Christian Liberal Arts College. Made possible through the generosity of Dr. and Mrs. Hugh A. White.
"Proud of the Past .... Confident for the Future"

Blake Glass (1978, left) and a fellow student have a relaxing conversation in front of the fountain and lamp at Centennial Gardens. This campus landmark is situated between Ormston Hall to the east, the advancement office to the south, and Dietzman Hall to the north. This is one of the central meeting locations on campus, where students congregate and where professors occasionally hold impromptu outdoor classes. According to an article in the Jackson *Citizen Patriot*, early plans included "a device for an eternal flame to be lighted in event the gas shortage ends." Initially constructed with a fountain, the water was eventually replaced by a rock and flower garden. It was unclear if this change was due to continual plumbing challenges or to incessant pranking by students. Soap suds in the fountain was a common prank, as was filling the fountain with hundreds of orange goldfish.

Similar to earlier field service groups that began in 1948, Common Bond was a traveling musical group that represented SAC by performing contemporary music at churches, camps, and youth events across the United States and Canada. These members pictured in 1993–1994 are, from left to right, Derek Grams (1995), Ryan Young (1996), Candy Munger (1996), Ryan C. Cole (1995), Melody Acker (1998), Kent Brugger (1996), Diane Caron (1995), and Jennifer Kovacs (1994).

LeRoy Holton (1953, 1955) is the owner and president of Spring Arbor Lumber. He served on the alumni board and the board of trustees. Holton was awarded the 1987 Distinguished Service Award for his outstanding support of the educational mission of SAC. Through the generous support of the Holton family, SAU dedicated the Holton Health and Wellness Services Center in 2000.

Doug Hawkins (1970) works at the WSAE turntables in 1968. WSAE hit the airwaves on June 29, 1963, as a 10-watt college station. The station was designed with "the needs of the curriculum in music, speech and dramatics. It will also be used in teaching, and indirectly will serve the interests of the college and the community," according to the *Bulletin*. Harold Munn, who served on the board of trustees, had the vision for a radio station at SAC and filed the initial application with the FCC. Munn donated a 500-watt transmitter, some turntables, and mixing equipment to help get the student-run station off the ground. In 2005, the station rebranded as Home.FM. Even though it has expanded greatly (now a 3,900-watt station), it has remained true to its purpose as a training ground for SAU students.

Lucy Maddox worked intermittently between 1949 and 1953 as dean of women and taught English classes. She returned in 1962 as the library curriculum coordinator. She was instrumental in the process of becoming a four-year college and helped plan for the library building (in what is now Dietzman Hall). Maddox served as director of the library and professor of English until her passing in 1985.

Lucy's sister Esther Maddox served on the faculty for 36 years until she retired in 1992. She taught speech and drama, directed plays, and wrote and produced reader's theater. At her celebration of life service, it was noted that she directed 25 full-length dramas, 20 one-act plays, and 32 reader's theatre performances. She received the 1990 Leroy M. Lowell Award for excellence in employee service.

In 1929, Everett E. Ogle and his brother started an automobile dealership in Spring Arbor. Ogle Brothers Chevrolet Sales and Service occupied the southeast corner of Ogle Street and M-60. Everett served on the board of trustees for 20 years and received the 1984 SAC Distinguished Service Award. Ogle sold a 27-acre parcel to SAU that was important to the future development of campus, providing space for Lowell Hall, the president's house, Ogle Village, the tennis courts, the fieldhouse, and athletic fields. The Ogle Art Center uses the same building that housed the car dealership. In 2005, the 7,100-square-foot Ganton Art Gallery was added to the Ogle Art Center. When his wife passed away, part of her estate helped establish the college's Dorrice A. Ogle Dining Commons in the Kresge Student Center.

Since as early as the 1920s, intramural athletics have been a significant part of the student life experience. During most of the SAC years, intramural sports were organized as a house system, with teams formed around campus housing. In the photograph at left, Lisa Cochrane (1978) referees a 1975 women's intramural volleyball game as Anne Way (1977) looks on. Below, Beta III battles on the court with Ormston I in a 1975–1976 men's intramural basketball contest in the fieldhouse. Teams earned points based on their performance, culminating with an all-sport intramural champion crowned at the end of each academic year.

On August 1, 1979, Kenneth Coffman began his tenure as the 22nd president of SAC, serving until 1988. Coffman came to SAC from Oakland University, where he was the vice president of campus and student affairs. His time at SAC was known for increasing the enrollment by 40 percent and tripling the operating budget. When possible, it is customary for past presidents to attend the inauguration of a new president. On this occasion, three prior presidents gathered in front of the periodicals in the library. Pictured from left to right are Leroy Lowell, Roderick Smith, David McKenna (1949), and Kenneth Coffman. Together, the men in this photograph led the school through the better part of three decades. Lowell served from 1935 to 1944 and 1955 to 1957, eliminating the college's debt during the Depression years and World War II. Smith from 1957 to 1961 laid the foundation for becoming a four-year college, and McKenna ushered in the transition to a four-year school and helped pen the Concept during the years of 1961 to 1968.

Beth Voller (1937) hosts students at the Voller house. Her husband, Ellwood "Woody" Voller (1933, 1935), served as president from 1968 to 1979. Over the years, it has been common for students to be hosted in the president's residence, a practice continued by current president Brent Ellis and his wife, Christy Ellis, to this day. Pictured from left to right are Chris Bramley (1974), Voller, Donna Schuur (1978), and Becky Woll (1980). The Vollers came to SAC from Roberts Wesleyan College, where Woody Voller was president from 1957 to 1968. The Vollers became the first inhabitants of the president's residence, which was built after they came to Spring Arbor. Howard Snyder wrote that "The residence was patterned after the president's home the Vollers had used at Roberts Wesleyan College—a fine house built on the site of the long-time home of B.T. and Ellen Roberts."

Voller House is the SAU presidential residence. Home to the presidents and their families since 1968, the naming ceremony in 1994 honored its first residents, President Voller and his family. Pictured from left to right are Cheryl Trepus, Martin Trepus, David Hamilton, Carolee Hamilton, and Beth Voller (1937). David and Carolee served on the faculty for three decades as dean of education and director of developmental education, respectively.

Members of the 1992–1993 SAC Student Association are, from left to right, (first row) Wes Stevenson (1995), Brian Dumont (1994), Matt Gray (1994), Dawn Foster (1993), and Rod Coxon (1993); (second row) advisor Jon Kulaga (1984, current president of Indiana Wesleyan University), Sally Ingles (1994), Pam Johnson (1994), Christina Sachau (1995), Robyn Rupp (1995), April Miller (1993), and David Barron (1993); (third row) Brad Wilcox (1994), Debbie Howard (1995), and Tim McAboy (1994).

In 1981, Ron Kopicko (1977) returned to SAC as student discipleship coordinator. His role evolved over the years, eventually becoming university chaplain. His impact during his 38 years on students and the spiritual culture of campus was immeasurable. From leading chapel, Sunday school classes, and Wednesday evening "By the Book" sessions, to 22 spring break mission trips, Kopicko tirelessly invested in the spiritual lives of students until his retirement in 2019.

Celestine "Sally" Trevan came to Spring Arbor in 1941 at the invitation of the president to join the faculty. Over her 34-year career at Spring Arbor, she taught high school, junior college, and college courses in history, English, and etiquette. She was recognized in 1986 with the Leroy M. Lowell Award for excellence in employee service. A campus Koinonia house is named after her.

Chapel is an integral part of the SAC experience, as shown in the 1988 photograph above. There have been two major "moving of the spirit" revival-type moments documented during the institution's history. In January 1956, a men's evening prayer meeting grew in attendance and lasted until four in the morning. The next day at chapel, the Spirit continued to work, with services and prayer gatherings continuing throughout the week. At halftime of a home basketball game, students spontaneously started singing hymns "much to the surprise of the visiting players," as reported in the *Bulletin*. The second of these movements was on April 24, 1995, when an invitation was given to come to the altar following a chapel message. This lasted for over four hours and continued into evening gatherings that lasted into the wee hours of the morning the following two nights. These spontaneous gatherings concluded at the next scheduled chapel service.

BULLETIN

Vol. 36   March, 1956   No. 1

A Cappella Choir In Spring Tour

A full schedule of concerts is being arranged for the A Cappella Choir, as preparations are begun for the spring tour. Thirty-six singers, under the direction of Mary Ruth Crown, will bring to a score of churches in Michigan and Ohio some of the blessing and joy they have

Revival Sweeps Campus

"When He Is Come"

January 17, 1956, as a date, will not be remembered by many, but the events of that day will live in the memory of scores of students and faculty members of our college for years to come. It was the day when God began to visit the campus in a succession of indescribable and unforgettable manifestations of His presence and power.

For want of a better name, this movement of the Holy Spirit in our midst has been referred to as "the revival." But it was no ordinary series of meetings. In fact, church services had little to do with it. Things broke into the open in a Tuesday morning chapel hour, and for nearly a week the regular schedule—classes, meals, athletics—gave way to God's working.

What took place was not entirely without warning. Stirrings of something unusual had been evident in some classrooms and dormitories. On Monday night before the eventful Tuesday, a small prayer meeting in the Men's Hall, scheduled for the usual course of a few minutes, grew in size and length until nearly half the dormitory was involved, with

It Was God

What took place was unmistakably the work of the Lord. With a bit of heaven dropped to earth, the unearthly was inevitable. But because it was of God, it was marked by beauty, order, and fitness. More than one

The 2002–2003 student association president Geila Rajaee (2003, left) and Ben Kreisch (2003, right) receive an ivy cutting at graduation. Students receive a cutting during freshman move-in weekend and another at graduation. The two leaves in the current university seal represent strength and stability and remind students of their ivy cutting ceremonies.

SAC celebrated its 125th anniversary in 1998. Cutting the anniversary cake are Pres. James L. Chapman (1951, 1954) and his wife, Mary. Chapman served as president from 1997 to 2000. Passionate about SAC and Jesus Christ, when speaking in chapel, he often became emotional while preaching on the mission of SAC. Chapman was instrumental in securing funding for the White Library and the Chapman Welcome Center, which sports his name.

Five

SPRING ARBOR
UNIVERSITY

In the fall of 1999, the SAC board of trustees voted to approve the process to secure university status. On April 30, 2001, university status became official. The announcement was made by Pres. Gayle Beebe in a special chapel service. The announcement was followed by a campus picnic and a balloon launch.

Shortly after achieving university status, a new logo (left) was designed to be used for athletics at Spring Arbor University. This logo was adopted in the 2002–2003 academic year. SAU updated its athletic logo in the 2017–2018 academic year (below). According to sports information director Chris Bauman, "Our goal was to develop a complete and unifying brand identity that not only honors our rich tradition but is a powerful representation of who we are and who we aspire to be." (See chapter six for previous logos and mascots.)

The graduating class of 2005 witnessed the dedication of the McKenna Carillon Tower on May 14, 2005. It was named to honor former president and chairman of the board of trustees David McKenna (1949). McKenna was an original drafter of the Concept, which is engraved below the tower. Each of the four planks of the Concept are represented on the side of the tower: total commitment to Jesus Christ, critical participation in the contemporary world, lifelong involvement in the liberal arts, and a community of learners. On each corner is etched a component of the Wesleyan Quadrilateral: scripture, tradition, reason, and experience. The tower provides a convenient waypoint when helping visitors navigate campus.

The need for a new library building had been growing for a number of years, with plans beginning in the early 1990s. Due to funding challenges, a new building was postponed. Hugh A. White's name adorned the previous library building (now Dietzman Hall). The Hugh A. and Edna C. White Library opened in January 2002. Edna White, who served tirelessly alongside her husband, was equally honored in the naming of the new library. With 40,000 square feet of space and the capacity to double its current print collection, this facility was a significantly upgraded resource befitting a newly christened university.

Hanging of the Greens is a tradition that began in 2001. Since Pres. Gayle Beebe and his wife, Pam, moved from California to Spring Arbor and were unaccustomed to Michigan winters, they desired to end the fall semester with a celebration of Christmas. Hanging of the Greens often includes fireworks, concerts, candle lighting, Christmas cookie decorating, and occasionally a haphazard live nativity by the men of Ormston Hall.

Camp Michindoh is a 250-acre Christian camp and conference center near Hillsdale, Michigan. In 2009, under the leadership of Pres. Charles Webb (1969), Camp Michindoh was gifted to SAU by the Orville and Ruth Merillat Foundation. At the time, it was the largest legacy gift to the university.

During the leadership of Pres. Brent Ellis, 2020 saw significant upgrades and renovations to campus entrances, including the completion of a new front gate. This main gate to campus received a new look with a wrought-iron and stone arch. To a visitor facing north from M-60, the new gate frames the E.P. Hart Circle. According to President Ellis, this landmark, erected in 2016, stands to "honor Hart's dedication to spiritually-integrated learning"—a commitment still honored to this day, 150 years later.

Six

ATHLETICS AT "THE ARBOR"

Deb Kuntzleman (1985) rounds a turn in a fall 1984 cross-country meet as the Spring Arbor College Cougar cheers her on in the background. Kuntzleman was an All-American in the National Christian College Athletic Association (NCCAA) in 1983 and 1984. She still holds the school best time in the marathon distance.

Donald "Mac" McDonald (1931, 1933) began coaching the Spring Arbor High School basketball team in 1948. The 1954 team pictured here is, from left to right, (first row) E. Andrews (1955, 1957), B. Barkwill (1954, 1956), F. Whims (1955, 1957), D. Young (1957), and L. Ganton (1954, 1956); (second row) manager D. Voller, J. York, F. Dawson, R. Krause, B. Pike (1955), N. Find, J. Wiedefeld (1954, 1956), D. Heimburger (1954, 1956), L. Zents (1955), G. Holton (1957, 1967), J. Sipes (1955), and Coach MacDonald.

Loved by all in the community, Mac McDonald was described in the 1951 yearbook: "Who but 'Mac' can coach a team, teach mathematics, and keep the home fires burning at the same time? Who but 'Mac' plays basketball in his sleep?" The athletic fieldhouse recently underwent a $1.9-million renovation and was named the McDonald Athletic Center, "the MAC."

Pictured is the 1952 SAHS basketball team. From left to right are (first row) Ron Robart (1952, 1955), Sid Chapman (1952) with Trigger the dog, Sam Ulsaker (1952, 1954), Don Jones (1952, 1954), and Bob Delamarter (1953, 1955); (second row) Coach McDonald, John Collins (1953), Lloyd Payne (1953), Charles Terman (1953), Bill Barkwill (1954, 1956), Larry Gorton, Duane Young (1957), Fred Whims (1955, 1957), Lloyd Ganton (1954, 1956), Ward Sipes (1952, 1954, 1980), and Carl Jacobson (1952, 1954).

Tony Mifsud (1963) is pictured on the inside lane running alongside Barry May (1965). Mifsud came to Spring Arbor Junior College as a high school all-American runner having posted the third fastest mile time in Michigan in 1962. At SAJC, he was the 1962 national community college cross-country champion. After graduating from SAJC, Mifsud went on to attend Eastern Michigan University, where he was a three-time NCAA All-American.

At some point in the 1940s or 1950s, the blue jay became the mascot of choice for SAJC sports. It is unclear when the mascot was initially adopted; the first print reference to it is in the 1950 school newspaper. Pictured here is a group of 1950s cheerleaders with the blue jay mascot on their sweaters.

SPRING ARBOR COLLEGE

COUGAR

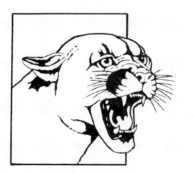

BASEBALL

1984 MEDIA GUIDE

In 1967, with the growth of athletics at SAC, a new mascot was deemed necessary. SAC teams were "known for their peak physical condition, their quickness and their tenacity," according to the *Bulletin*. Despite the reputation of blue jays as fierce, aggressive birds known for their protective territorial behavior, it was put to a student vote, and "Cougars" was chosen. Sports fans were encouraged to cheer "Chew 'em up, Cougars!"

Sue Pifer (1980) laces up her cleats as she prepares to take the softball field. Pifer was a member of the inaugural softball team at SAC. Softball was added as an intercollegiate sport in the 1976–1977 academic year.

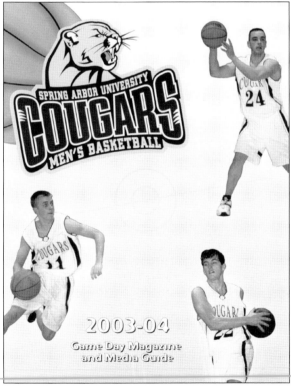

Micah Lancaster (2006) is the career assists leader for men's basketball and a member of the 2,000-Point Club. Lancaster (No. 11) led the team to two NCCAA national titles in 2005 and 2006. A two-time National Association of Intercollegiate Athletics (NAIA) All-American, Lancaster started his own basketball skill development training company working with college and NBA players. He recently appeared in the Netflix film *Hustle*. Pictured with him are Michael Folkert (No. 22, 2006), and Ryan Walter (No. 24, 2004).

The men's cross-country team competes in a fall 1992 race. Pictured from back to front are Chris DeBacker (1995), Jacob Snyder (1997), and Brian Teed (1996). DeBacker is on the SAU top-10 record list for the indoor track and field 600 and 800 meter events.

In this mid-1970s photograph, members of the men's cross-country team are, from left to right, David Luke (1977), Robert Gould (1976), Brad Buter (1977), John Rose (1976), and Marc Willis (1974). Willis is on the SAU top-10 record list in the outdoor track and field 400 meters and indoor 1,000 meters. Gould currently serves on the SAU board of trustees.

Ted Comden served Spring Arbor University as professor of exercise and sport science from 1968 to 2003. He was recruited to come to SAU by friend and former teammate Hank Burbridge. Comden coached both men's and women's cross-country teams as well as the men's track and field team. SAU alum and former runner Don Walker (1978) said of his coach, "I saw firsthand many times just what a class act he was (and is) and was reminded of what a great decision it was to come to Spring Arbor." In addition to being inducted into the SAU Athletic Hall of Fame for coaching in 1999, Comden was named the 1987 recipient of the Leroy M. Lowell Award for his excellence in employee service and contributions to the educational ministry of SAC. The Comden Courts in the campus fieldhouse are named in his honor.

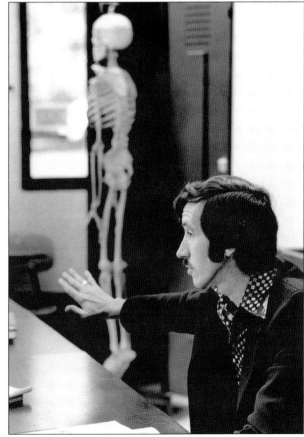

One of the limited opportunities for athletic participation for women until the 1970s was cheerleading. Pictured in this early 1960s photograph in the original campus gym are, from left to right, Beth McDonald (1961), Ann Short (1962), Irene Youngfrau (1960, 1962), Karen Boileau (1960, 1966, 1996), and Beverly Dunckel (1965).

In this image, the 1973–1974 SAC cheerleaders set up in a pyramid-style pose on the athletic field. From left to right are (first row) Diane Martz (1977); (second row) Barbara Watts (1976), Cindy Whited (1977), and Gayle Lusher (1975); (third row) Phyllis Carlson (1977).

While the cheer team at SAC was named the "Cougarettes," at times, men participated in cheer at SAU. The 1991 team is, from left to right, Chris Brown (1992), Holly Taylor (1994), Trent Wilson (1992), Kristi Dengler (1992), Kathy Burkhart (1994), Chad Cole (1995), Stacy Walters (1992), Andy Hughes (2005), Stacy Guscinnski (1992), Niki Peters (1995), Eric Campbell (2003), and Dale Killinger (1992).

Here, the 1995–1996 SAC Cougarettes pose in front of the Centennial Gardens fountain. From left to right are (first row) Jenna Mauer (1998), Sadie Marx (1997), and Stephanie Smith (1997); (second row) Amanda Foley (1999), Cristi Martinson (1999), and Tari Thompson (1999).

A 1959 SAHS graduate, Kay Dunckel went on to complete degrees at Seattle Pacific University and Eastern Michigan University before returning to Spring Arbor in 1972. From 1972 to 2005, she served as an assistant professor of physical education and associate athletic director, and coached volleyball and women's basketball. Dunckel was instrumental in championing for equal opportunities for women in athletics at Spring Arbor. She advocated that women should be awarded athletic scholarships, just like men, and for commensurate team budgets and pay for women's coaches, insisting that uniforms be provided for women's teams. The Dunckel Gymnasium in the campus fieldhouse is named in her honor. In addition to being inducted into the SAU Athletic Hall of Fame for coaching in 1996, she was named the 1993 recipient of the Leroy M. Lowell Award for excellence in employee service and contributions to the educational ministry of SAC.

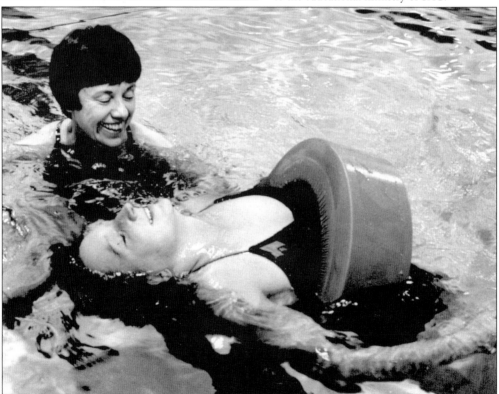

Courtney Thompson (1999) prepares to shoot a free throw against Benedictine University. Thompson, inducted into the SAU Athletic Hall of Fame in 2005, is one of the most decorated basketball players in SAU's history. She holds records for most points in a career, rebounds in a season, blocks in a game/season/career, and career triple-doubles. She also holds the record for most games played and was an NAIA All-American in 1999.

The 1989–1990 women's basketball team is, from left to right, (first row) Sherry Claypool (1994), Susan Kersten (1990), Shari Anderson (2010), Stacy Thomas (1990), Angie Lindteigen (1990), Karrie Braun (1990), and Amy Nolan (1993): (second row) assistant coach Lois Peck (1989), Tracy Regal (1992), Sandi Bremiller (1992), Vicki Renefar (1990), Kim Merillat (1993), Chris Piziali (1992), Jill Chaney (1990), Nicole Mayer (1993), and head coaches Kay (1959) and Darrell Dunckel (1967).

This undated photograph from the first half of the 20th century shows students playing tennis on a dirt court in front of the old administration building. Tennis did not become an intercollegiate sport at SAC until the 1960s. The administration building, dedicated in 1905, served as a multipurpose facility. The tennis court area would later become the Centennial Gardens.

Bob Beardslee (1979) attempts a backhand during the 1975 season. The tennis team was led to a 5-2 record that season by coach Charlie Carey. Carey started the tennis program and coached from 1964 to 1979. He was a professor of mathematics from 1964 to 2013, retiring after 49 years because, as he stated, "49 is a perfect square." He received the Leroy M. Lowell Award in 1995 for excellence in employee service.

Deb Thompson (1984) became head softball coach in 1987. Over the past 35 years, she has amassed more than 800 wins. She led the team to the NCCAA national title in 2005, the same year she was named NCCAA Coach of the Year. In addition to being inducted into the SAU Athletic Hall of Fame for coaching in 2002, Thompson was the 2010 recipient of the Leroy M. Lowell Award for excellence in employee service and contributions to the educational ministry of SAU. She has taught exercise and sport science since 1989. In 2021, the NCCAA renamed its annual award for Christian character in softball the Deb Thompson Award. To quote the awards description, Thompson "is the embodiment of a Christian coach, who serves selflessly while nurturing those student-athletes who have had the benefit of calling her coach."

Kerry Hettinger (1983) wrestles his Grand Rapids Baptist Bible College opponent to the mat. SAC fielded an intercollegiate wrestling team for a few years in the late 1970s and early 1980s. In recent years, SAU has added new co-ed varsity sports like bowling and competitive cheer as well as women's golf.

The golf program started in 1989. One player short to field a team that first season, coach Bill Bockwitz recruited Beth Puckey (1993) to join the men's team (women's golf started in 2016). The team won NCCAA championships from 1994 to 1996. Pictured is the fall 1996 team. From left to right are Corey Casler (2000), Jason Colter (2004), Kevin Kilgore (1997), Jason Swihart (1996), Jason Stiles (1996), Brian Stucky (2000), David Page (1999), and Jeff Swihart (1999).

Bill Bockwitz served as an associate professor of physical education from 1965 to 1968 and 1972 to 1999. He was inducted into the SAU Athletic Hall of Fame for coaching in 1997. Bockwitz coached basketball, cross-country, and track and field, and he started the golf program. He led the men's golf team to four NCCAA national championships during his 17 years at the helm and was the NCCAA Coach of the Year from 1995 to 1998. In 2000, Bockwitz received the Leroy M. Lowell Award for his excellence in employee service and contributions to the educational ministry of SAC.

Paul Lynch (1954, 1956) was one of Spring Arbor's first African American graduates. Born into a religious family as one of nine children, Lynch came to Spring Arbor from Shreveport, Louisiana. He starred in track and cross-country at Spring Arbor. Upon graduating, he went to law school, eventually working as an assistant US attorney and later a district court judge in Louisiana. Lynch was so highly regarded as a man of character in the legal community that at the time of his passing, the Shreveport Bar Association eulogized: "The hand of God didn't shake when he made Paul Lynch. We fear we shall not soon see his like again." Pictured from left to right below are Charles Terman (1953), Don Jones (1952, 1954), Ward Sipes (1952, 1953, 1980), and Lynch.

Meran Miles (2001) hands the baton to Kelli DeCamp (1999) during a 1998 indoor track meet. Miles and DeCamp are two of the more dominant runners in SAU history. Both were NAIA and NCCAA All-Americans and are in the top 11 cross-country times ever posted at SAU. DeCamp still holds the SAU 3,000-meter record, while Miles's indoor 800-meter record was only recently bested by Jaydn Fuerst (2020).

SAC offered women's tennis as a varsity sport for the first time in 1991. The 1993 team pictured here finished second in District 23 and third in the conference tournament. From left to right are (first row) Joy Salow (1993), Lora Van Wieren (1995), Michelle Mogg (1994), and Amy Smith (1994); (second row) coach Steve Schippers (1987), Leina Royston (1995), Jennifer Moore (1995), and Evie Buchholz (1994).

Verdon Dunckel, or "Uncle Dunk" as he was affectionately known by students, had a diverse career at Spring Arbor. He served as chaplain from 1964 to 1981. Before that, he was the college pastor at the Spring Arbor Free Methodist Church. Dunckel was on hand to minister to students during the campus revival in January 1956. In addition to serving the college as the director of counseling, he became the soccer coach in 1971. Dunckel was recognized in 1977 with the SAC Distinguished Service Award. He, along with his wife, Bernadine, who also worked at the college, were recognized as recipients of the 1997 Leroy M. Lowell Award for their excellence in employee service and contributions to the educational ministry of SAC.

Michelle Redman, senior cocaptain of the 1991–1992 volleyball team, gets ready to serve during a fall 1991 game. The team won 29 games that season and finished second in District 23. Redman was named a member of the District All-American team.

The 1989–1990 women's volleyball team is, from left to right, (first row) Carol Ruder (1993), Michelle Redman (1992), Barb Brewer (1991), Kim Austin (1991), and Kim Merrillat (1993); (second row) Kristen Nowlin (1991), Lisa Owen (2007), Angie Williams (1993), Susan Kersten (1990), Kelly Ransom (1991), Dina Hopkins (1990), and coach Stan Gibbs (1978). Team captain Kelly Ransom was NAIA All-District Honorable Mention that season.

Jack "Jackie" Evans is arguably the greatest scorer in the history of SAU men's basketball. Evans's name litters the SAU basketball record book. His 61 points in a single game is a mark that still stands. During the 1972–1973 season, he set the SAU record for most points in a season, 1,003. The 1973 *Converse Basketball Yearbook* listed Evans as the top scorer in all of college basketball. He also holds SAU records for highest points per game average for a season (34.5 in 1972–1973) and career (30.3 1971–1973), most made field goals in a game (24) and season (380), and most free throws made in a game (19) and season (243). After his time at SAC, he was drafted by the NBA's Baltimore Bullets.

A 2003 inductee into the American Baseball Coaches Association Hall of Fame, Hank Burbridge coached the baseball team from 1964 to 2004. During that time, he notched 1,003 wins against 519 losses. In 2004, Burbridge was named NAIA Coach of the Year. His reputation as a man of character and his Christian witness were so evident that the NAIA created the Hank Burbridge Champions of Character Award to recognize a baseball player displaying exemplary character and sportsmanship. Burbridge took his teams to the NCCAA national tournament 29 times, winning the title on four occasions. The NCCAA created the Hank Burbridge Award to recognize a player for Christian service through baseball. The SAU baseball field is named in his honor. Pictured from left to right below are Theron Spence (1975), Burbridge, and Ken Klinger (1977).

Under the leadership of coach Craig Hayward (1972) and assistant coach Marci Piper (1983), women's soccer was offered as a varsity sport for the first time in the fall of 1992. Pictured here is Tina Hayward (1997), a member of one of the first varsity women's soccer teams at SAC in a 1994 match.

The 1995 women's soccer team is, from left to right, (first row) Pam Thompson (1996), Jill Busen (1995), Mary Stelzer (1995), Marcie Ellison (1995), Amy Marlett (1997), Laura Underwood (1996), and Tammy Adkins (1996); (second row) coach Craig Hayward (1972), Janette Thompson (1995), Melody Cox (1996), Yolanda Willis (1998), Heidi Lake (1997), Rachele Warner (1995), Jodi Johnson (1997), Charlotte Hicks (1996), Tina Hayward (1997), and assistant coach Marci Piper (1983).

Yolanda Willis (1998) comes out of goal in a fall 1996 game to punt the ball toward the opposing team's goal. In recent years, SAU women's soccer has become a dominant force in the NAIA, appearing in the national tournament every year since 2010 and winning national titles in 2015, 2017, and 2022.

Jason Crist (1998) has been at the helm of women's soccer at SAU for more than 20 years. Crist, an SAC men's varsity soccer player, has turned SAU women's soccer into an NAIA powerhouse. He led the team to three NAIA national titles and has coached 49 NAIA All-Americans, including three National Players of the Year. In 2022, he became the winningest women's soccer coach in NAIA history. In addition to his coaching duties, Crist was named athletic director in 2023.

For more than four decades, Terry Darling (1978) led the tennis program at Spring Arbor University. After playing as a student, Darling took over the head coaching duties from Charlie Carey in 1980 at the age of 23. The son of psychology professor Harold Darling, he led the men's team to more than 400 victories. He was conference coach of the year in 1997, 1999, 2006, and 2011, achieving NAIA Region VIII Coach of the Year honors in 2007. He was inducted into the SAU Athletic Hall of Fame in 2013. In addition to coaching tennis, Darling has served as a professor of psychology since 1980. In 2000, Darling received the Leroy M. Lowell Award for his excellence in employee service and contributions to the educational ministry of SAC. In 2022, Darling retired as head tennis coach and was succeeded by his son David (2013).

Bob Briner served as the first athletic director from 1962 to 1964. He is seen here addressing the 1963–1964 men's basketball team, which he coached. Briner went on to become an Emmy-award-winning television producer and sports management executive. He is the author of numerous books, including his influential *Roaring Lambs*. This book had a significant impact on how evangelical Christians could be culture-shapers.

For almost a quarter of a century, Ryan Cottingham (1994) has been on the sidelines leading the men's basketball program. Cottingham, an NAIA All-American as a player, coached the team to NCCAA titles in 2005 and 2006 and an NAIA championship in 2019. He is the all-time career wins leader in men's basketball at SAU, recently surpassing the 400-win mark.

The 1977 men's soccer team was ranked fourth in the NAIA. With a 19-0 record, they were the only undefeated team in the country, and had the nation's highest goal scorer that season, Howard "Brit" Taylor (1979). The final playoffs were scheduled for November 27—a Sunday. At the time, SAC had a long-standing policy of not participating in athletic events on Sundays for religious reasons.

The 1977 captain, Blake Glass (1978), rises above the crowd to win the ball. Despite the best efforts of SAC officials requesting a schedule change, the NAIA refused. As a result, coach Phil Bartlett and the team withdrew from the finals rather than play on Sunday. According to the *Journal*, when Pres. Ellwood Voller announced the college's decision in a student assembly, his students gave him a standing ovation.

Howard "Brit" Taylor (1979) powers a goal into the back of the net. Taylor, whose father was a minister, came to SAC from Lancashire, England, after his family hosted an SAC student. After his experience hosting a student from this small school in Michigan, Taylor decided to bring his goal-scoring prowess to SAC. His 35 goals led to him being named NAIA Honorable Mention in 1977.

The sophomores won a mid-1930s women's intramural basketball class tournament. Pictured from left to right are (first row) Bethavery Smith (1937); (second row) Lorraine Dowley (1935, 1937), Erma Rowe (1937), Margaret Paquette (1937), Charlotte Phillips (1937), Ruth Baker (1935, 1937), and Velma Williamson (1935, 1937).

Bibliography

Blews, Richard R. *Master Workmen: Biographies of the Late Bishops of the Free Methodist Church During Her First Century: 1860–1960*. Wilmore, KY: First Fruits Press, 2016.

Cunningham, Beverly. *Spring Arbor Township: 1830–2013*. Spring Arbor, MI: Saltbox Press, 2013.

Journal (1975–present; 1927–1970 as *Bulletin*, 1970–1975 as *Update*). Spring Arbor, MI: Spring Arbor University. library.arbor.edu/c.php?g=840780&p=6011972.

Kulaga, Jon S. *Edward Payson Hart: The Second Man of Free Methodism*. Spring Arbor, MI: Spring Arbor University Press, 2007.

Light + Life (1970–present; 1868–1970 as *The Free Methodist*). Indianapolis, IN: Light + Life Publications.

Michigan Conference of the Free Methodist Church Annual Conference Minutes. library.arbor.edu/c.php?g=840780&p=8206912.

Ormston Hall Men's Residence Photograph Collection. Spring Arbor University Archives. library.arbor.edu/c.php?g=840780&p=8078716.

Snyder, Howard A. *Concept and Commitment: A History of Spring Arbor University: 1873–2007*. Spring Arbor, MI: Spring Arbor University Press, 2008.

Spring Arbor University Athletics. https://saucougars.com/.

The Spring Arbor Chronicle, 1897–1908, Spring Arbor, MI.

The Spring Arbor University Concept

Spring Arbor University is a community of learners distinguished by our lifelong involvement in the study and application of the liberal arts, total commitment to Jesus Christ as the perspective for learning, and critical participation in the contemporary world.

Discover Thousands of Local History Books
Featuring Millions of Vintage Images

Arcadia Publishing, the leading local history publisher in the United States, is committed to making history accessible and meaningful through publishing books that celebrate and preserve the heritage of America's people and places.

Find more books like this at
www.arcadiapublishing.com

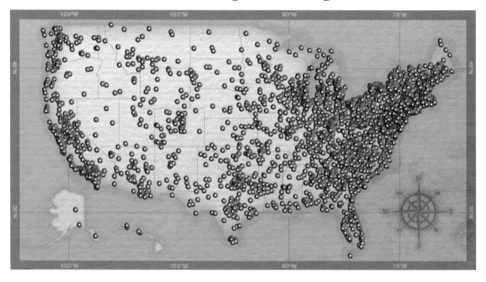

Search for your hometown history, your old stomping grounds, and even your favorite sports team.

Consistent with our mission to preserve history on a local level, this book was printed in South Carolina on American-made paper and manufactured entirely in the United States. Products carrying the accredited Forest Stewardship Council (FSC) label are printed on 100 percent FSC-certified paper.

MADE IN THE USA